CRAFTS
OF THE ANCIENT WORLD

THE CRAFTS AND CULTURE OF
THE ANCIENT GREEKS

Joann Jovinelly and Jason Netelkos

the rosen publishing group's
rosen central

To Eden Willow

Published in 2002 by The Rosen Publishing Group, Inc.
29 East 21st Street, New York, NY 10010

First Edition

Library of Congress Cataloging-in-Publication Data

Jovinelly, Joann.
The crafts and culture of the ancient Greeks / Joann Jovinelly and Jason Netelkos.
p. cm. — (Crafts of the ancient world)
Includes bibliographical references and index.
Summary: Describes easy-to-make crafts that replicate the arts of ancient Greece. Includes historical material, a timeline, a glossary, and resources.
ISBN 0-8239-3510-8
1. Greece—Civilization—To 146 B.C.—Juvenile literature. 2. Creative activities and seat work—Juvenile literature. [1. Greece—Civilization—To 146 B.C. 2. Handicraft—Greece.]
I. Title. II. Series.
DF78 .J68 2001
938—dc21

2001004717

Manufactured in the United States of America

Note to Parents
Some of these projects require tools or materials that can be dangerous if used improperly. Adult supervision will be necessary when projects require the use of a craft knife, an oven, a stovetop, plaster of paris, or pins and needles. Before starting any of the projects in this book, you may want to cover your work area with newspaper or plastic. In addition, we recommend using a piece of thick cardboard to protect surfaces while cutting with craft or mat knives. Parents, we encourage you to discuss safety with your children and note in advance which projects may require your supervision.

CONTENTS

In many instances, the attitudes that shaped ancient Greece are familiar to us because they have formed the foundation of modern Western civilization. Ancient Greece was a vital culture, active and individualistic. It helped define an ideal of Western beauty in all artistic pursuits, including painting, writing, and, perhaps most important, architecture.

The culture of the ancient Greeks, created during a golden era of achievement that lasted about 2,000 years, is divided into three separate periods. The first of these is referred to variously as the Great Bronze Age, the Minoan Period, or the Age of Heroes. Spanning from about 3000 BC to 1100 BC, the earliest Greek peoples—the Minoans and their successors, the Mycenaeans—settled and cultivated the islands off the Greek coast in the Aegean and Adriatic Seas. Although these scattered settlements sometimes united to defend their

The earliest Greeks, the Minoans, settled islands off the Greek coast.

territories against common enemies such as the Persians, for the most part they remained self-sufficient city-states. Each prayed to its own patron god, and worship of these gods seems to have been central to the thought and activity of the Minoan and Mycenaean civilizations.

The first of these settlements was built on the island of Crete and reached its peak between 2200 BC and 1450 BC. It was enriched economically and culturally through trade with other Greek islands, Egypt, and Syria. These Cretan settlers, the Minoans, were named for King Minos. Minos was said to be the son of Zeus, king of the gods, and the human woman Europa. Legend states that he became king of Crete with the help of Poseidon, king of the seas. Minos established a navy, gained control over the Aegean Islands, and colonized them with Cretans. His wife, Pasiphae, daughter of the Sun, gave birth to the

This is a map of ancient Greece and its colonies.

Minotaur, a half-bull, half-human figure. He was housed in the Labyrinth, a
palace composed of thousands of wind-
ing passages. Most accounts describe
Minos as a powerful and just ruler (giv-
ing Crete its earliest set of laws), but
some legends claim he fed Athenian
children to the Minotaur as revenge for
the murder of one of his sons by the
Athenians. The civilization named for
Minos prospered, and palaces, including
Minos's palace, have been found in
many of the ancient sites in the cities of
Knossos, Zakro, Phaistos, and Mallia.

The Mycenaeans resided in several
city-states, each with its own king. One
of the most famous of these rulers was
Agamemnon. He helped his people
become great warriors and dominate the
Minoans. The Mycenaeans tried to
defend their territory against enemies by
building huge walls around their palaces
and towns. Eventually, however, they
were conquered by the Dorians from the
Balkans. By 1200 BC, most traces of the
Mycenaean people had vanished. A
period known as the Dark Ages in
ancient Greek history had begun.

The stories of both the Mycenaean
and Minoan civilizations were kept alive
by Greek storytellers. Storytelling is an
art that was popular in most ancient

cultures. Two of these famous stories, or epic poems, as they are now known, *The Iliad* and *The Odyssey*, have survived because they were written down in the eighth century BC by a famous Greek poet named Homer. They relate some tales of the Trojan War, including fierce battles for the ownership of the abandoned and destroyed lands of the earlier Mycenaean civilization and of the ancient city of Troy.

During the Dark Ages in Greece, small and distant city-states—known then as polis—began to develop slowly and prosper. Each consisted of a central town or village and surrounding farmland. Most were built around a hill or a cliff called an acropolis (high place of the city), and each had its own government. It is in this era, beginning in 650 BC—the Archaic period—when the founding of many small and separate city-states occurred, that the power of ancient Greece was established once more.

Eventually, two major city-states emerged as the civilization's most successful new centers of power and influence: Athens, a port city known for its distinctive accomplishments in the arts, and Sparta, a place where the fiercest Greek warriors were trained. Known as the Classic Age, it was a time that would forever symbolize the high level of artistic and militaristic accomplishment for

which ancient Greek civilization would later be remembered.

DAILY LIFE

As in most ancient cultures, home and family formed the core of Greek civilization. Large, close-knit families often lived under the same roof, along with slaves or hired servants. Generally, the homes or villas were modest in size, normally no more than one or two private rooms in addition to the main living quarters.

Nearly every home was made of mud bricks, similar in style to that of Egyptian homes of the same period, and built on a simple stone foundation. Every home also contained a small indoor altar for the purpose of worshiping the gods, and an outdoor statue meant to protect the premises from evil spirits (usually a bust of Hermes, the patron god of travelers). The roofs were covered in baked tiles that allowed rainwater to fall from them evenly. Since the Greeks cherished privacy, most homes contained only small open windows situated near the roof that could be closed with wooden shutters. Some homes had bathrooms with small tubs for bathing, and smaller basins for washing the hands and face. The first showers were invented by the Greeks and popularized by their athletes. Showering usually occurred only in public bathhouses.

The male master of the household had the largest bedroom and the nicest furniture. His wife was forbidden to use specific rooms, such as the andron (where the master of the household entertained male guests), and she often enjoyed very few luxuries. It was deemed morally proper for Greek women to be separated from men in most public and social situations. Often the only times that men and women mingled were during religious festivals, at family functions such as weddings, and at the theater. Most marriages were arranged for political or financial reasons, so many couples did not necessarily want to spend a lot of time in each other's company. Still, falling in love was not uncommon, and it was often the subject of many Greek plays of the day.

A woman's life was considered more important if she gave birth to a male child who would continue the family bloodline. Sometimes, if a father chose not to keep an infant, the baby would be left outside to die. These infants were sometimes taken in by others and raised as slaves. If, by the tenth day, a child remained in the care of his or her parents, he or she would be named and accepted into the family. Girls never attended school and were raised by their mothers, learning how to keep a home and preparing for marriage by the age of thirteen or fourteen. Boys were expected to learn how to read, write, do arithmetic, master a musical instrument, and study poetry and literature. Education for boys usually ended around the age of thirteen or fourteen. If they wanted to continue beyond this age, they were offered higher education by traveling educators called sophists.

BELIEFS

The Greeks were pagans, or non-Christians. They believed in numerous gods whom they worshiped by offering various sacrifices on the altars of the many temples they erected. Some of these temples, many of which are still standing, reveal to archaeologists and

Greek women are depicted bathing a child in this carving from an ancient theater in Perge.

This tile mosaic from Pompeii shows the famous Greek philosopher Plato with a group of his students.

offerings if one wanted to ensure good fortune and health.

Great thinkers from the ancient world, such as the philosophers Plato, Aristotle, and Socrates, the poets Homer and Sappho, and the physician Hippocrates (to whom the Hippocratic oath is attributed), still speak to us today through their words, which have survived through the ages. Like young Greek boys who studied works written by these Greek masters, scholars today still examine and interpret these writings and regard them as an important component of their education and a valuable guide to the difficult moral, ethical, and philosophical questions of life.

Aristotle, a student of Plato, defined the Greek character by stressing the spiritual importance of nobility, a quality he divided into four major categories. The four categories, each considered a virtue, included courage, temperance, justice, and, most important, wisdom, or *sophia*. In order to be considered a man of noble character, according to the ancient Greeks, a man had to exhibit all four virtues with every action that he took.

historians much about what ancient Greek culture must have been like. Greeks believed that their gods and goddesses looked and behaved very much as they did, and to each god or goddess they attributed a specific area of influence. For example, Aphrodite was the goddess of love, Demeter was the goddess of the harvest, Persephone was the goddess of the underworld, Artemis was the goddess of hunting, and so on. These gods and goddesses were thought to be responsible for successes and failures, sickness and health, wealth and poverty. So they needed to be kept happy with

The Greeks also believed in physical ideals, such as health, strength, beauty, and wealth. The emphasis on physical and spiritual ideals reflects their respect for humanity and its vast potential. The ancient Greeks respected each individual person for the wisdom that he or she could impart. Each man, woman, and child was recognized as worthy and useful. This respect for the individual and his or her contributions to society formed the core of the Greek conception of democracy, which is the ancestor of our own form of government. It is for this reason that Greek civilization remains closely linked to our own.

WARFARE

During the summer months, when war often broke out, men were encouraged to volunteer to defend their city-state and often had to supply their own gear. Since the number of men who were willing to serve began to dwindle over time, the Greeks were forced to reconsider their methods of mustering troops. By the end of the fifth century BC, nearly every man between the ages of eighteen and sixty was expected to serve the war effort in some capacity.

A soldier's rank and duties often depended upon his economic and social status. The wealthiest men rode on horseback or served aboard ships. The middle-class soldiers traveled on foot. These soldiers were known as hoplites, and each hoplite had a slave to carry his seventy pounds of gear.

Arranged in an orderly formation called a phalanx, these men would fight their enemies at very close range, or as one Greek poet explained, "toe to toe and shield against shield." Normally, battles were won or lost quickly. If they survived, farmers could soon return to their families.

Men from the city-state of Sparta were more prepared for any war effort and were much more disciplined fighters than soldiers from Athens. Boys from Sparta were recruited into the military at the age of seven and forced to forage for their own food, swim in ice cold waters, march barefoot, and constantly engage in brutal, hand-to-hand combat. These activities took place in a boarding school environment and served to transform boys into resourceful men and fierce warriors. Unlike in Athens, serving in the Spartan militia was a full-time occupation. Its harsh discipline came to characterize all of Spartan society. When we use the adjective "spartan" today (meaning self-denial and self-discipline, or being simple or spare), we are actually hearkening back to the severe lifestyle of Sparta's warriors.

Generally, conflicts between the Greek city-states were brief, contained, and usually devoted to disrupting the local economy and work force. The war effort reached another level, however,

On the left, an actor is dressed in a Spartan military helmet. On the right, a painting shows a line of heavily armed soldiers, known as a phalanx.

when the ancient Greeks fought the Persians (490–478 BC) and opened up a massive land and sea war. The same was true of the Peloponnesian War (432–404 BC) between Athens, Sparta, and various allies of both city-states. Historians believe that the sophisticated style of warfare later used by Alexander the Great to conquer all of Greece, Egypt, and Rome, was first developed during these two extended wars.

LANGUAGE

Everyone equates the style of writing known as hieroglyphic script with the Egyptian civilization, but few know that the Greek alphabet was preceded by the use of a system of symbols similar to Egypt's hieroglyphs. The earliest Greeks, the Minoans, developed a system of hieroglyphs referred to by linguists as Linear A. It is thought to be directly related to Egyptian script. With Linear A, each letter was symbolized by an animal or object. Later, Mycenaean palace scribes would take the language one step further, creating syllable groups that formed words. This new script is referred to as Linear B and is considered the earliest form of the Greek language.

Although Greek was in use, it was still in an early stage of development. Its dialect and alphabet varied from region to region. By the sixth century BC, the Greek language was known and used throughout the Mediterranean, and communication, writing, and education began to spread.

ART

Of all ancient civilizations, Greece is among the most celebrated for its artistic achievements. Greek innovations in architecture, sculpture, and crafts, such as pottery, continue to define our notions of beauty. The work of craftspeople in such fields as gem cutting, ivory carving, jewelry making, and metalworking still awe and inspire us today.

The Greeks were the first ancient civilization to sculpt in a naturalistic style, meaning that the human figures looked almost real. This style is known as Archaic. A female statue was called a kore, and male statues were known as kouros. Many represented gods, warriors, and athletes. We think of Greek sculptures being all white, but they were in fact painted in bright colors, which are now completely worn away.

Art was an important pastime for the Greeks. A great many men and women were employed as artisans, and for the first time in history art was being collected and appreciated

The ancient Greeks continue to influence modern societies. Their architectural styles are evident even in the United States Supreme Court building in Washington, D.C.

by people in their homes. Prior to this time, art was mostly viewed in public places. Greek leader Alexander the Great was an enthusiastic and respected art collector. In addition to maintaining a staff of artists, Alexander managed to collect some of the most striking sculptures produced by Greek artisans.

Warfare

I n the epic poem *The Odyssey*, the Greek poet Homer tells the story of Odysseus, a man who suffers many trials and setbacks in his attempt to get home to his wife and son following the end of the Trojan War, an adventurous journey that lasts ten years. Our term "odyssey," which refers to a very long trip full of lots of diversions and detours, is derived from the name of Homer's hero. Homer's other great epic poem, *The Iliad*, describes the long, bloody struggle between Greek and Trojan soldiers, such as Achilles and Hector. The Trojan War, fought in 1200 BC by the Mycenaeans, and led by King Agamemnon, was long thought to belong only to the realm of myth until archaeologists unearthed the actual site of Troy (in northwest Asia Minor) and physical evidence of a violent destruction dating from the years in question.

The ancient story of the Trojan horse centers on an ingenious trick. The Greeks constructed a giant wooden horse, filled it with soldiers, and left it outside the gates of the city of Troy. The

These are ruins of the southeastern Tower of Troy, now in modern-day Turkey.

Trojans, figuring the long siege of their city was over after they watched the Greeks sail away in their boats, pulled the giant horse within the walls of their city, thinking it was a gift. Then, late that night, the Greek soldiers who were hidden inside the belly of the horse opened the gates to the city and united with the rest of their army that had been waiting silently on the shore. As the story goes, the Greeks then destroyed the city of Troy and gained control of its wealth. The story of the Trojan horse inspired the proverb we often hear today, "Beware of Greeks bearing gifts."

This is an image of Ajax defending Greek ships against the Trojans.

A modern replica of the Trojan horse stands in the city of Troy today. Like the original, this one is also made of wood. But today, children, not soldiers, climb into and out of its belly.

This is a replica of the Trojan horse in Troy. The Greeks used the horse as a container to secretly carry their troops into the city.

Trojan Horse

What will you hide inside the belly of your Trojan horse?

YOU WILL NEED
- Large, empty salt container
- Small, empty food boxes
- Two cardboard paper towel rolls
- Masking tape
- Scissors
- Bottle caps or buttons
- Craft paint
- Paintbrush
- Black construction paper

Step 1
Cut a paper towel roll in half. Cut five small slits along both ends of each tube. Fold back the cuts to create flaps. Tape the flaps of the tubes to your salt container, one tube at each end of the container. These two tubes represent your horse's legs. Tape the tube's bottom flaps to a small recycled box. This is the horse's base.

Step 2
To make the horse's head and neck, cut an additional paper towel roll, approximately half the size of the legs. Make slits along the bottom to attach it to the salt container. This will be the neck. With additional cardboard, cut out the shape of your horse's head. Tape it to the neck.

Step 3
Cut slits along the bottom of a small box. Tape them to the back end of the horse's body. Tape a folded piece of cardboard to the box to make a peaked roof.

Step 4
To give your horse a wooden appearance, apply strips of masking tape to its entire surface and base. Add ears and a mane to your horse by attaching small pieces of cut cardboard to its head and neck with tape.

Step 5
Glue buttons or bottle caps to the sides of the base to serve as its wheels.

Step 6
Paint your horse. When it dries, glue small, black squares to its sides for windows.

Festivals and Celebrations

Festivals held to honor gods and goddesses in ancient Greece usually included sacrifices and a feast for everyone who attended. Many also featured popular music of the day, public processions, and chariot racing.

The greatest festival of all, the Panathenaea, was held every four years and lasted for six days. The celebration united all of the people of Athens, who marched to the summit of the acropolis. Many carried clothing with them up the steps of the Parthenon, the city's main temple, and into its interior as offerings to the goddess Athena. The festival included all sorts of events, such as athletic competitions, and tremendous amounts of food, music, and dancing.

Other festivals included the Olympic Games, first held to honor the god Zeus in 776 BC. The very first Olympics included competitions still present in the modern games, such as foot racing, horse racing, javelin hurling, discus throwing, and wrestling. Women were forbidden from watching the games, many of which were played in

This is a Roman copy of a Greek statue of Myron of Athens. Discus throwing was one of the original events in the ancient Olympics and is still featured in the modern games.

the nude. Discipline in the Greek sporting events was strict, and many rules applied to the men who competed.

One of the most popular festivals in Greece was held to celebrate Dionysus, the god of the vine and fertility, during which Greek theater was traditionally celebrated. An annual festival that opened in late March, it featured productions of new Greek plays that were written for the season. These works included both comedies and tragedies that showcased the struggle, sorrow, and humor of the human condition. Plays were written by such masters as Aeschylus, Sophocles, and Euripides.

These are the ruins of the third century BC Greek theater at Epidaurus. It was made of limestone and held 14,000 spectators.

Greek theater was a unique art form of its day. The concept of performed recreations of scenes from life, history, or mythology originated in Athens in the sixth century BC and was immediately popular. Shortly after the first public performances, Greek theater evolved to include more elaborate trappings, such as costumes, scenery, tickets to enter the arena, and awards for its best actors. There were even street vendors available who sold food that was prepared in portable kitchens outside the theater during some performances.

Greek theater was supported by private donations and taxes, and the theater festival, featuring up to eighteen performances, attracted financial backers to fund the productions. A theater investor of this sort was known as a *choregus*.

This is a Hellenistic tragic theater mask.

Comedy and Tragedy Masks

Organize your very own festival to honor the god Dionysus. Make several masks and put on a play.

YOU WILL NEED
- Sawdust
- Cornstarch
- Powdered alum
- String
- Craft knife
- Craft paints
- Yarn, fur, beads
- Pencil
- Paintbrush
- Saucepan
- Baking sheet
- Water

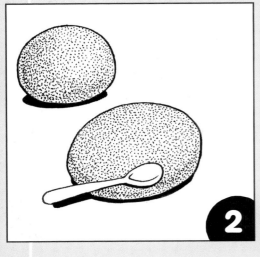

Sawdust Clay Recipe
2 cups sawdust
1 cup cornstarch
2 teaspoons powdered alum
1 cup of hot water

Combine all dry ingredients in a large saucepan. Add the water and cook over low heat. Stir constantly for about five minutes, or until the mixture becomes thick and heavy. Remove from the heat and scoop the clay onto a baking sheet to cool before modeling.

Step 1
Make a batch of sawdust clay using the recipe on this page.

Step 2
Divide the clay in half. Roll both halves into balls. Flatten the two halves into circular shapes, as shown.

4

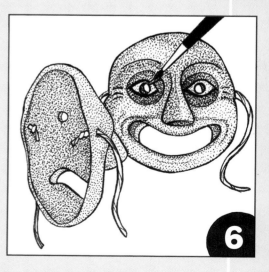

5

6

Step 3

Use your finger to make two holes in your masks for your eyes. Cut a mouth in each mask and remove the excess clay. If you wish, use this clay to sculpt noses or ears using simple shapes.

Step 4

After sculpting, make two holes, using a pencil point, on the edges of both masks, as shown. Set the masks in a sunny window for two to three days, or until completely dry. Turn them over after the second day, so that they dry evenly.

Step 5

Paint your masks with craft paint. Add fur, yarn, or other accessories as you wish.

Step 6

Thread strings through the holes in the sides of your masks so that you can wear them. Now you're ready for a starring role in a Greek play!

Science and Education

The Greeks were among the most intellectually and scientifically advanced civilizations in history. One of the earliest Greek scientists, Thales of Miletus, successfully predicted a solar eclipse long before the invention of the telescope or other means of studying the cosmos. Pythagoras of Samos was a famous and respected mathematician who is still as influential today as he was 2,500 years ago. He is credited with the development of the Pythagorean theorem, an important geometry formula, and with the creation of musical scales. Greek astronomer Aristarchus understood that Earth revolved around the Sun hundreds of years before this truth was generally accepted.

Another famous Greek scholar is Hippocrates, the physician who is described as the father of modern medicine. He is known for writing the Hippocratic oath that all doctors take before practicing. Some of the earliest known works of science and literature

The Greek god of medicine, Asclepius, treats a patient in this stone carving.

have been traced back to ancient Greek authors. Hippocrates himself penned fifty-three books about medical topics, which are now collectively known as the Corpus.

Even with all of their advanced understanding of science and medicine, the Greeks still blamed the gods for disease. They even believed that Asclepius, the Greek god of medicine, would appear to them in their dreams

20

to prescribe certain treatments such as diets or herbal remedies. Many afflicted Greeks spent the night on the altar steps, hoping for the gods to take mercy on them and cure them of their ailments. In keeping with these beliefs, temple sanctuaries for the sick have been identified all over the islands of Greece, as well as on the mainland.

A poet reads from a scroll as his student listens.

Given their accomplishments in the arts and sciences, it is no wonder that the Greeks considered education a top priority for young boys. Though many attended school from the age of seven, older boys were often taught by traveling teachers called sophists, or "wisdom-sellers." Making their living by teaching grammar, mathematics, geography, and public speaking, sophists often took advantage of youths hungry for knowledge and eager to compete in the world. Unlike philosophers such as Socrates, Plato, and Aristotle, who offered free lessons and believed it unethical to charge money for educating the youth, the sophists demanded payment. By the fourth century, however, most teenage males spent two years in state schools known as gymnasiums.

This is a Roman abacus, similar in style to the Greek abacus. Both are early types of calculators.

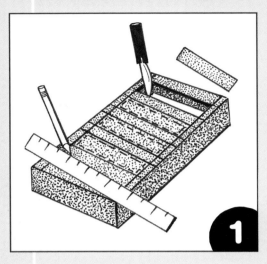

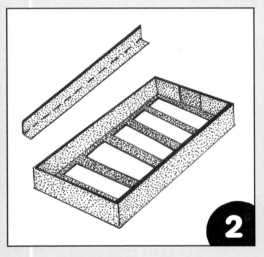

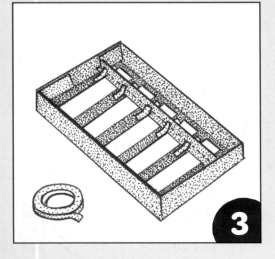

Greek Abacus*

Many young Greek boys used an abacus to help them with their math problems the way we now use calculators. Construct an abacus, and give the old-fashioned way a try.

* ADULT SUPERVISION IS REQUIRED FOR THIS CRAFT.

YOU WILL NEED
- **Cardboard shoebox lid**
- **Craft knife**
- **String**
- **Buttons or beads**
- **Recycled cardboard scraps**
- **Ruler**
- **Craft paint**
- **Hole puncher**
- **Tape**
- **Paintbrush**

Step 1
Using the edge of a ruler, draw narrow rectangles across the width of the inside of your shoebox lid. Make the rectangles approximately 1/2 inch wide and 4 inches long. Separate each rectangle with a 1/2-inch space, as shown. Carefully cut out each rectangular section with a craft knife.

Step 2
Cut a strip two inches wide from a piece of cardboard that is long enough to run the length of the shoebox lid from top to bottom. Fold a 1/2-inch edge along the strip's entire length.

Step 3
Tape the strip, running lengthwise, on the inside of your shoebox lid.

Step 4
Use a hole puncher to make holes along both lengths of your box edge. These holes should be positioned at every row of cut rectangle shapes. Punch corresponding holes in the taped strip as well.

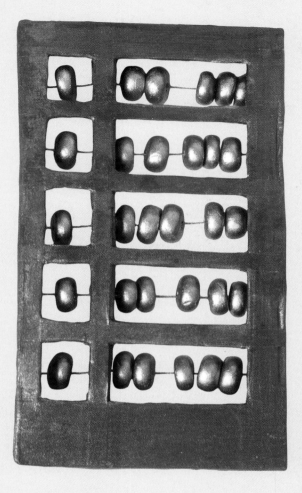

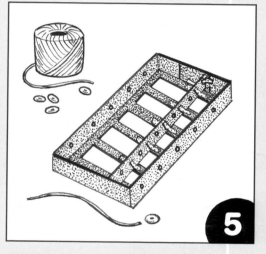

Step 5

Thread a long string through each hole on one side and out the opposite side. Thread buttons or beads on the strings from both ends. The cardboard strip in the center will separate the buttons.

Step 6

Once your buttons or beads are strung, tie the strings in knots at each hole. Now, paint the front of your abacus. The number of buttons or beads you use will depend on the size of your shoebox. (For information on how to use an abacus, consult an encyclopedia or go to http://www.beatthecalculator.com.)

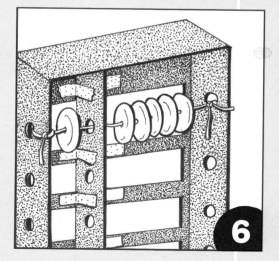

Art and Leisure

This ancient Roman painting depicts knucklebone players.

Those ancient Greeks who were wealthy and owned slaves were among the first people in history able to enjoy the time and freedom for leisure activities, such as theater, sporting events, music, bathhouses, or dinner parties with friends. Games were popular, too, such as knucklebones (a game for women that was similar to jacks), spinning tops, an early form of backgammon, chess, and a drinking game called kottabos. The object of kottabos—to hit a specific target with drops of wine flicked from a drinking cup—was difficult for some to achieve, as the game was usually played during a drinking party, or symposia, after much wine was consumed.

The wives of the men who attended these drinking parties were not invited, but slave girls, who knew special dance routines and could play music for the small crowd, often entertained the revelers instead. Usually these parties became more and more rowdy as the night wore on, until the men drank too much and fell asleep, leaving a large mess to be cleaned up.

Other leisurely entertainments, often enjoyed only by the wealthiest Greeks, included listening to music.

Songs were central to activities of all kinds, including births, funerals, times of harvest, and times of war. Although men and women played instruments, only women danced.

Music was often created with stringed instruments such as the lyre, which was made of wood, ivory, or tortoise shell and fitted with strings made from animal innards. The kithara and the harp were other popular stringed instruments. Percussion and wind instruments were represented by the syrinx and the panpipe. Even those people with limited musical talent could have enjoyed castanets (small cymbals made of bronze), drums, or tambourines.

Poetry was often recited as an accompaniment to live music. This was so commonplace, in fact, that boys were expected to play an instrument in school. Boys also learned stanzas of poetry by heart.

The Greeks attributed special powers to music. Even Plato said that music was an art that inspired virtue in the soul. Unfortunately, no one is certain how ancient Greek music sounded, since none has survived.

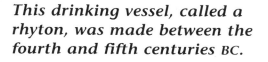

This drinking vessel, called a rhyton, was made between the fourth and fifth centuries BC.

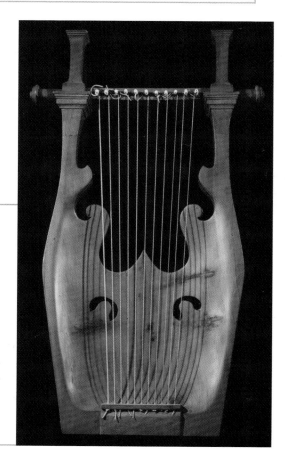

This is a replica of a lyre, an ancient stringed instrument. It was an important element in Greek music, dance, and poetry.

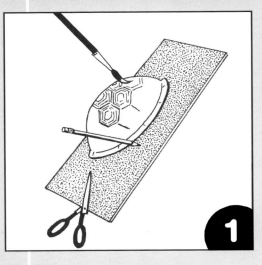

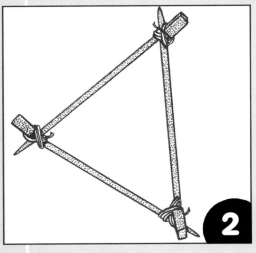

Tortoise Lyre

Memorize a few lines of your favorite poem, create this simple lyre, and pretend to play along with your recited verses.

YOU WILL NEED
- **Paper bowl**
- **Scissors**
- **Hole puncher**
- **Paper fasteners**
- **Large rubber bands**
- **Recycled cardboard**
- **Popsicle stick**
- **Three chopsticks**
- **String**
- **Masking tape**
- **White glue**
- **Craft paint**
- **Permanent markers**
- **Paintbrush**
- **Pen or pencil for tracing**

Step 1
Paint your paper bowl to resemble a tortoise shell. Be imaginative when decorating your shell. When the paint is dry, trace the rim of the bowl onto a piece of cardboard. Cut out the circle. This will be the bottom of the tortoise shell.

Step 2
Tie three wooden chopsticks together with string. Use plenty of string to tie them, forming a triangle. Knot the strings securely.

Step 3
Tape a point of the triangle to the center of the cardboard circle. Securely tape the sticks to the edge of the cardboard as shown.

Step 4

Lay the tortoise shell on top of the cardboard and draw an arched line around the two exposed chopsticks. Cut out this line so the shell rests over the sticks. Punch holes along the rim of the shell and through the cardboard with a hole puncher. Join the shell and cardboard together with paper fasteners.

Step 5

Cut four or five rubber bands in half. Cut slits along the exposed edge of the cardboard as shown.

Step 6

Tie the ends of the rubber bands to the chopstick. Make a knot in the opposite end of each rubber band. Wedge the knot into the slits. Glue a Popsicle stick along the edge of the bowl to keep the wedged knots in place. Your lyre is ready to play!

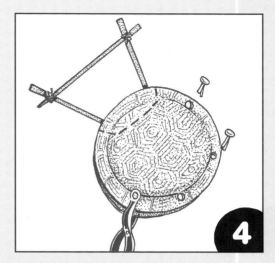

4

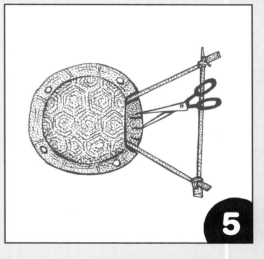

5

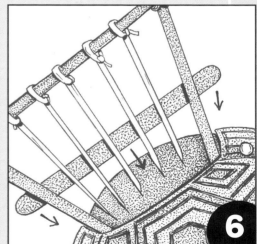

6

Art and Architecture

The most famous of the Greek ruins, the temple known as the Parthenon, still stands on a summit in the modern city of Athens. It was once dedicated to Athena, the goddess of war and wisdom. Standing tall as Athens' contribution to the Golden Age of Greece, the Parthenon is situated alongside two smaller temples, the Erechtheum (whose columns—carved in the shape of female figures called caryatids—supported its roof) and the Temple of Wingless Victory (dedicated to Athena), both built between 421 and 405 BC.

As a public building that all Athenians were free to use and admire, the Parthenon was more than a religious symbol for the city's people during the height of the Classical Age. The temple stood as a reminder of Greek potential, of industry, and of an architectural mastery that still mesmerizes the world today.

The temple, considered an almost perfect example of architectural

This Roman statue of Athena Promachos was based on the Greek original.

proportion and symmetry by modern architects, is actually an optical illusion, altered in scale to improve imperfections in human vision and meant to be seen from a distance. Because columned and rectangular or square buildings tend to look top heavy, the

Parthenon's columns were designed so that they were thinner at the top than at the middle, making the temple's upper reaches appear to be lighter and airier. The columns were constructed in the Doric style. Eight columns filled the front and back and seventeen made up each side.

This is a pediment from the temple of Zeus.

Designed by two architects named Ictinus and Callicrates, the Parthenon featured beautiful pediments (the triangular top of the temple that rests on the columns) that depicted the birth of Athena on one side and her conflicts with the god Poseidon on the other. A frieze (a long, mural-like sculpture that is carved into a flat surface) wrapped the entire perimeter of the temple and depicted scenes from daily life in Athens. Inside the cella, the long front interior chamber, was the actual sculpture of Athena, designed by Phidias. She stood more than forty feet high and was covered in more than 2,500 pounds of gold. Her arms were made of ivory, and she beckoned all Athenians to stand at her feet and worship.

In 1687, the Parthenon was almost destroyed when gunpowder that was stored inside the temple exploded. Though a near complete ruin today, the Parthenon remains one of Greece's most popular attractions.

The Parthenon, beloved by both ancient and modern Greeks

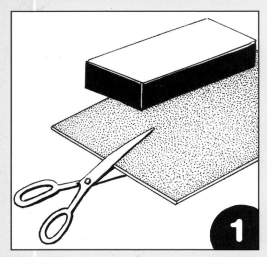

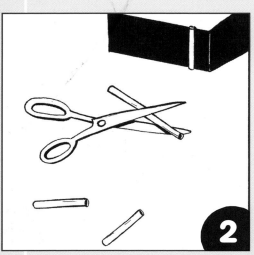

The Parthenon

Design a treasure box constructed in the style of the ancient Parthenon.

YOU WILL NEED
- Small rectangular box
- Recycled cardboard
- Plastic drinking straws
- Ruler
- White glue
- Scissors
- Craft paint
- Paintbrush
- Tape

Step 1
Cut a piece of cardboard slightly larger than the bottom of your empty rectangular box. This is the base of your Parthenon. Paint the box black and the cardboard base white. Set both aside to dry.

Step 2
Cut drinking straws the same size as the height of the box. Cut as many straws as you will need to place around the sides of the box at evenly-spaced intervals. These straws will serve as the "columns" of the Parthenon. Paint each one white.

Step 3
Glue the bottom of the black box to the white base. Glue the drinking straw pieces to the sides of the box, leaving an equal space (about the width of a straw) between each column.

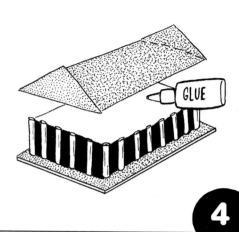

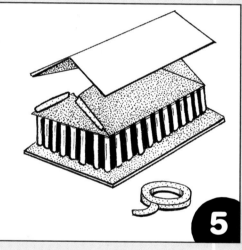

Step 4
Using a ruler, draw a rectangle on a piece of cardboard the same size as your box top and cut it out. Tape triangles to the sides, as shown. This piece will be the roof and pediments. Glue the roof to the top of the Parthenon.

Step 5
Cut a rectangle approximately the same size as the Parthenon's base. Fold it in half lengthwise so that the folded edge forms the top of the roof's peak. Glue it to the ceiling and pediments.

Step 6
When the glue has dried, add additional details by drawing figures on the pediments with a pen or with paint.

Decorative Arts

Wealthy Greek women lived very sheltered lives. They spent much of their day indoors looking after their homes and often found time to devote to their appearance. They were particularly fond of jewelry of all kinds. Almost any type of jewelry—earrings, bracelets, or necklaces—could have been found on wealthy Greek women of the ancient world, most of it gold or enameled. Some designs were detailed and sophisticated. Others were plain and simple. Some of the most elaborately designed jewelry has been found in the ancient city of Troy.

Women enhanced their appearances in a number of other ways, too. One of the most common methods was the use of cosmetics imported from Egypt. Fashions of the day dictated that women, especially in Athens, keep their skin as pale as possible. Pale skin was a kind of status symbol, since only wealthy women could remain indoors all day without having to leave the house to work or shop for food. In order to conform to this fashion trend, many

Pictures of women often appeared on their possessions, such as this cosmetic box.

women lightened their faces with white lead powder, without knowing that the substance was actually highly toxic, or poisonous. Historians have speculated that the use of white lead powder contributed to the fall of the Roman Empire, since lead poisoning can lead to brain damage. Greek women used other cosmetics and toiletries, such as perfumes, myrrh, eye pencils and shadows, blush, lotions, and olive oil to keep their bodies glistening and moist in the hot, dry climate.

Hairstyles were also important to Greek women, especially if they were going to be attending a special wedding or festival. Normally, a woman's hair was always worn long but was usually pulled up and away from the face and held in place by a headband, ribbons, nets, or scarves. Sometimes, a lock of hair was removed and offered to the gods as a sacrifice, especially before a ceremony such as a wedding. Cut strands were also displayed as a sign of mourning.

Early Greek hairstyles included braids and curls. In later times, the hair was tied back with gold and silver headdresses, bands of bronze, or special netting. Appearance was a high priority for Greek women in the ancient world, and the many artifacts that archaeologists have found related to female beautification are a testament to that fact.

Like modern women, Greek women wore their hair in a variety of styles, depending on the trend of the moment.

These Greek golden earrings incorporate a charm in the shape of a woman's head.

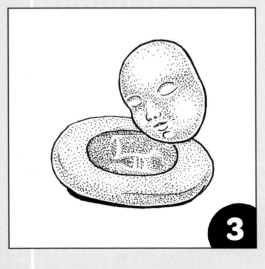

Greek Jewelry

The Greeks were inspired to design jewelry in natural shapes, such as snakes, birds, or the human body.

YOU WILL NEED
- Self-hardening clay
- Toothpicks
- String
- Craft paint
- Paintbrush
- Miscellaneous objects (such as small doll heads, for making the charm molds)

Step 1
To make a mold for jewelry charms and interesting beads, roll lumps of clay into balls. Flatten the balls into patties.

Step 2
Make imprints in the clay using various small items such as the head of a small, poseable doll or action figure. Allow the clay mold to dry and harden.

Step 3
Once your mold is dry, press small lumps of clay into it. Remove the clay.

Step 4
Turn the clay cast into a bead by inserting a toothpick through it. Reuse the molds to make many beads for a necklace or a bracelet. Make plain beads, too, by rolling small balls and sticking a toothpick through them.

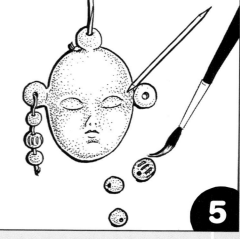

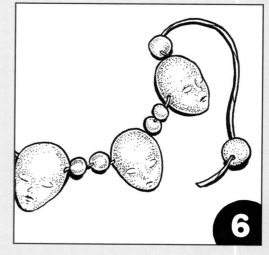

Step 5

To make a fanciful charm, attach a small bead to each side of a head bead using a toothpick. When dry, string smaller beads from the sides of the head to make earrings.

Step 6

Once your beads have dried, paint them with metallic gold paint. After the paint has dried, thread your beads on a piece of string. Knot the ends to form a loop so you can wear it around your neck or your wrist.

Religion and Beliefs

Greeks formulated their opinions about religion based on how they viewed themselves and their place in the world. Because they felt that the gods regarded them with interest, Greeks elevated and celebrated themselves in their worship. Some of this self-regard stems from Greek ideas about beauty, and the fact that they equated beauty with health, and health with approval from the gods. Greeks often had strong beliefs in their own outward beauty and unfailing strength. That is why Greeks who were ill often requested that the gods heal them; to be the most healthy, the most strong, and the most beautiful was the highest ideal in ancient Greek society.

In order to ask the gods for health, strength, and beauty, you had to first please the gods. As a result, prayer and sacrifice went hand-in-hand when Greeks approached a temple altar.

A Greek actress dressed as a high priestess lights a cauldron at the Temple of Hera of ancient Olympia during a rehearsal for the Olympics.

According to legend, different gods preferred different offerings of food and drink. To this day, we often hear the expression, "I'll leave it for the gods," when someone doesn't finish eating the food on his or her plate. The simplest sacrifice, a libation, was merely a pouring of wine on the altar itself. Animals were another common sacrifice.

Some Greeks left votives, or tokens, on the altar as an offering to the gods. Usually created for a specific purpose and meant to attract the attention of a specific god, these small offerings often took the form of marble (or, in modern Greece, embossed metal squares) which would be left behind on the altar when the worshiping had commenced.

These votives were also meant to be interpreted as a way to give thanks to the gods for healing or curing the sick or afflicted. Sometimes a specific part of the body was modeled in metal; for instance, a person who was thankful for a healed broken limb may have left behind a model or a token of that limb. This idea of creating a token of thanks continues as a tradition in Greece to this day. Set on display for short periods of time, votives could also be offered to the gods when a person felt as if he or she may have violated a religious custom. Occasionally, worshippers would be asked to bring votives to the altar as a service to the temples. Most were discarded soon after the ritual offering, but some marble statuettes were sometimes left as permanent fixtures in the temple by wealthy private owners or city-states.

A cow is led to sacrifice in this image from the Parthenon.

This is a carving of a youth making an offering to the Ludovisi Throne.

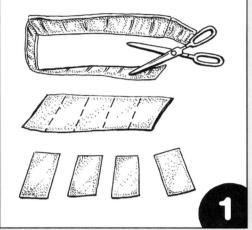

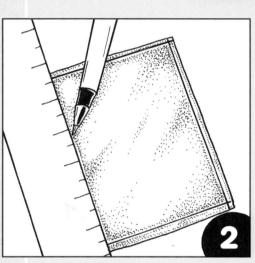

Votives

Thanking the gods was something that the ancient Greeks did on a daily basis. You too can make votives to commemorate special occasions or celebrate some good luck you have received.

YOU WILL NEED
- **Aluminum foil baking tray**
- **Ballpoint pen**
- **Scissors**
- **Toothpicks**
- **String**
- **Hole puncher**

Step 1
Cut and remove the bottom of your aluminum foil baking tray. Be careful; the edges will be sharp. Divide the foil piece into sections, each section representing a single votive.

Step 2
Using a ruler, draw a narrow border around your foil cutout. Press firmly with a ballpoint pen to make the frame.

Step 3
With a toothpick or a pen, draw a basic outline of your design. Note the raised image in the foil on the reverse side.

Step 4
Color in areas you want to emboss. If you make a mistake, you can smooth the foil on the reverse side with a toothpick.

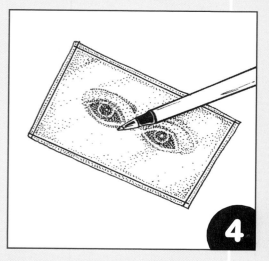

4

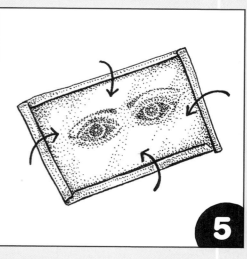

5

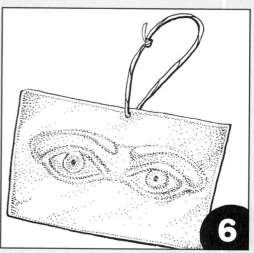

6

Step 5

When your design is complete, fold the edges of the frame over the drawn side of your token. This will remove the sharp edge.

Step 6

To hang your tokens, carefully puncture a hole at the top using a hole puncher or the tip of your pen. Tie a piece of string through the hole to make a loop.

Craftspeople

Craftspeople flourished in the cities of Greece, from stone carvers, blacksmiths, and jewelers to shoemakers, weavers, and basketmakers. Their workshops could be found in the center of town and people from all over the city and beyond would come by to examine and purchase their products. The marketplaces were busy, and merchants from the surrounding areas would mix with local farmers who would arrive to sell vegetables, fruit, and cheese. Other people bustled around, too, making the marketplace all the more hectic. Slaves waiting to be sold stood on platforms in the summer heat; dancers and acrobats milled around, performing for small change; and traders from surrounding cities sought good bargains on items of value.

Among the items available for trading were olive oil, olives, wine, metalwork, and, most important, pottery, a Greek specialty. Nearly every town in Greece contained what was then called a potter's quarter—a *keramikos*—

Greek potters at work are depicted on this bowl.

where pottery of all kinds would be made and exported to other areas for sale. The styles depicted on pottery are typical of the civilization between 1000 and 500 BC. Most of these designs depicted daily life in Athens and other city-states and were available in many shapes and sizes depending on what was being stored in them. This pottery provides us with a valuable glimpse into how the Greeks lived, dressed, and enjoyed themselves as well as how they viewed important events of the time such as war, famine, or plague. Most feature silhouettes in black or red figures, and some include griffins—mythical monsters which had lions' bodies and eagles' heads. Handmade with the help of manual pottery wheels, pieces of Greek pottery were beautiful and highly sought.

This pottery, or earthenware, had many uses other than storage of wine, water, or oil. Roof tiles and children's toys, for example, were often made of earthenware. Made from terra-cotta, an Italian term which means "baked earth," the Greeks mastered the art of working with pottery in a short time and became known for their use of the distinctive red Athenian clays. The red and orange tones commonly seen on Greek pottery were formed by controlling the amount of oxygen in the kiln (oven) where the clay was fired (baked).

Very little was wasted in ancient Greece; any material that could be reused was. Broken bits of pottery, for example, were often used as writing boards to post messages and announcements.

This ancient Greek relief depicts women dancing.

This black figure amphora, or large jar, could be used to store liquids.

Black and Red Pottery

Design your very own earthenware pot like the ancient Athenians did thousands of years ago.

YOU WILL NEED
- White glue
- Water
- Newspaper
- A round balloon
- Masking tape
- Recycled cardboard
- Aluminum foil
- Scissors
- Black and orange craft paint
- Paintbrush

Step 1
Make a water and glue solution by mixing three parts glue to one part water. Blow up your balloon and tie it securely. You do not need to fully inflate your balloon; make it as small or as large as you would like your vase to be. Tape cardboard rings to the top and bottom of the balloon with masking tape. Empty masking tape rings work best, but you could use taped cardboard strips to form rings, too.

Step 2
Dip strips of newspaper into the water and glue solution. Cover the entire surface of the balloon and the rings with six to eight layers of papier-mâché. Cover the inside of the bottom ring, too, but not the inside of the top ring. This will be the opening of your vase. Lay the vase upside down to dry overnight.

Step 3
Once your surface has dried and hardened, pop the balloon and remove it from the papier-mâché vase. Cut two pieces of aluminum foil (each about 10 inches long) and roll them both into tubes.

Step 4
Shape the tubes into handles and attach them to the sides of your vase with masking tape. Cover the handles and surrounding area of the vase with several layers of papier-mâché. Allow it to dry overnight.

Step 5
Paint a large orange circle in the center of your vase, and paint the surrounding areas black. Draw or paint your design (such as human figures or animals) within the circle. Look at pictures of Greek pottery for inspiration, or use your imagination.

Step 6
For a decorative border, follow the diagram in picture six to make a Greek key design.

TIMELINE

BC	**3500**	Egyptians develop first hieroglyphs.
	2575	Egypt's Old Kingdom begins. The Great Pyramids and the Sphinx in Giza are started.
	2040	Egypt's Middle Kingdom begins.
	1650	Mycenaean culture develops in Greece.
	1540	New Kingdom begins in Egypt.
	1333	Tutankhamen rules over Egypt and brings back the worship of many gods.
	1163	King Ramses III, the last great pharaoh of Egypt, dies.
	1070	New Kingdom ends. Attackers seize area and divide it in two. Egypt loses power.
	776	First Olympic Games in Greece.
	550	First Greek theater; Greek coins.
	500	Classical Age begins in Greece.
	490	Persians invade Greece, beginning the Persian War (490–478 BC).
	474	Building of the Parthenon begins.
	438	Building of the statue of Athena Parthenos begins.
	432	Parthenon complete.
	432	The beginning of the Peloponnesian War between Greece and Sparta. It ended in 404 BC.
	430	Great plague of Athens, Greece.
	425	Building of Temple of Athena Nike begins.
	336	Alexander the Great rules Greece.
	334	Alexander the Great invades Asia.
	332	Alexander the Great conquers Egypt.
	323	Alexander the Great dies. Greek Hellenistic period begins.
	264	The Punic Wars begin between the Roman Empire and the Carthaginian Empire of North Africa.
	147	Rome rules Greece.
	49	Julius Caesar rules Rome.

GLOSSARY

acropolis   Central hill in a Greek polis, or city-state.

amphorae   Large pottery jars for storing wine, sauce, or oil.

andron   Room in which the master of the house entertained his male guests.

archaeologist   Person who studies ancient civilizations by analyzing its objects.

Archaic Age   Historical period from 800 to 500 BC.

artifact   Object, especially a tool, made by human craftsmanship.

Bronze Age   Historical period lasting from 3000 to 1100 BC.

caryatid   Column that is designed as a female figure.

cella   Interior room within a temple where the statue of the temple's god is housed.

city-state   One of the small states that developed in ancient Greece, usually situated around a city or an island.

Classic Age   Historical period lasting from 500 to 300 BC.

colonnade   Row of columns.

Dark Age   Low point in ancient Greek history (beginning around 1200 BC) due to war, famine, poverty, and plague.

democracy   System of government in which people choose representatives to govern them.

Doric   Type of design, usually referring to column design.

drachma   Silver coin issued by the city of Athens.

fresco   Painting technique in which paint is applied to wet plaster. Most frescoes appear on walls.

frieze   Band of sculptures, often running around a Greek temple.

lyre   Ancient stringed instrument.

Minoans   Bronze Age Greeks who inhabited the city of Crete.

Mycenaeans   Bronze Age Greeks who succeeded the Minoans and took over the mainland.

Panathenaea   Athenian religious festival held every four years to honor the goddess Athena.

pediment   Triangular gable on the front and back of a Greek temple.

phalanx   Greek military formation in which hoplites, or foot soldiers, stand side by side and advance on the enemy.

polis   City-state.

symposium   Small dinner party, usually in a private home.

FOR MORE INFORMATION

ORGANIZATIONS

The Archaeological Institute of America
Boston University
656 Beacon Street
Boston, MA 02215
(617) 353-9361
Web site: http://www.archaeological.org

Dig! The Archaeology Magazine for Kids
30 Grove Street, Suite C
Peterborough, NH 03458
(800) 821-0115
Web site: http://www.digonsite.com

Metropolitan Museum of Art
1000 Fifth Avenue
New York, NY 10028
Web site: http://www.metmuseum.org

Smithsonian Institution Information Center
1000 Jefferson Drive SW
Washington, DC 20560-0010
(202) 357-2700
Web site: http://www.si.edu

World Archaeological Society
120 Lakewood Drive
Hollister, MO 65672
(417) 334-2377

In Canada

Ontario Archaeological Society
11099 Bathurst Street
Richmond Hill, ON L4C 0N2
Web site: http://www.ontarioarchaeology.on.ca

Royal Ontario Museum
100 Queen's Park
Toronto, ON M5S 2C6
Web site: http://www.rom.on.ca

WEB SITES

Odyssey Online
http://carlos.emory.edu

Online Exhibition of Greek and Roman Art (J. Paul Getty Museum of Art)
http://www.getty.edu/artsednet/resources/Beauty/index.html

FOR FURTHER READING

Crosher, Judith. *Technology in the Time of Ancient Greece.* San Diego, CA: Raintree/Steck-Vaughn, 1998.

Hart, Avery, and Paul Mantell. *Ancient Greece: 40 Hands-On Activities to Experience This Wonderous Age.* Charlotte, VT: Williamson Publishing Co., 1999.

Kerr, Daisy, and Mark Bergin. *Ancient Greeks.* New York: Franklin Watts, 1997.

Pearson, Anne. *Eyewitness: Ancient Greece.* New York: DK Publishing, 2000.

Steele, Philip. *Clothes and Crafts in Ancient Greece.* Milwaukee, WI: Gareth Stevens Publishing, 2000.

INDEX

ABOUT THE AUTHOR AND ILLUSTRATOR

Joann Jovinelly and Jason Netelkos have been working together on one project or another for more than a decade. This is their first collaborative series for young readers. They live in New York City.

PHOTO CREDITS

SERIES DESIGN AND LAYOUT

Evelyn Horovicz